DINOSAURS

book-studio

A DINOSAUR WORLD

What do you think of when you hear the word 'dinosaur'? Do you imagine a savage Tyrannosaurus Rex as tall as a house, with a huge mouth and slashing teeth? Or do you picture a lumbering Diplodocus stretching its long neck to reach the leaves of a tree? Maybe you think of the less obvious ones – the swift, running Coelophysis, the spiky, short-legged Stegosaurus or the duck-billed Parasaurolophu

DINOSAUR INVASION

In the beginning, there was no life at all on Earth. Firstly, microscopic bugs appeared; then, after millions of years, sea creatures and plants arrived. Much later, Earth saw a dinosaur invasion. The dinosaurs lived during a period of time called the Mesozoic Era. This era is split into three periods – Triassic, Jurassic and Cretaceous.

EARTH BREAKS APART

During the Mesozoic Era, Earth went through huge changes. The dinosaurs, and the environment they lived in, were dramatically affected by the altering planet. The land on Earth was joined in a huge mass called Pangaea which, over time, broke into smaller continents.

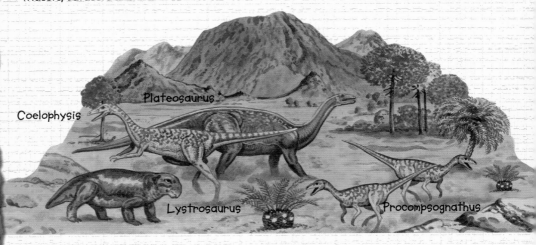

Coelophysis

Plateosaurus

Lystrosaurus

Procompsognathus

TRIASSIC PERIOD 248 million years ago

During the Triassic period the climate was warm and dry. Plant-eati dinosaurs gathered near the wetter coasts to feed on giant ferns. Small, swift meat-eaters hunted lizards in the inland deserts.

Brachiosaurus

Diplodocus

Allosaurus

Heterodontosaurus

Stegosaurus

JURASSIC PERIOD 206 MILLION YEARS AGO

Pangaea broke in two and the pieces drifted apart. Even so, there were some land bridges between the continents, which meant dinosaurs could walk between them. The movement of the continents affected Earth's climate. Temperatures fell slightly and rainfall increased – producing lush vegetation that grew over vast areas. The dinosaurs that fed on it grew, too.

Tyrannosaurus Rex

Struthiomimus

oplocephalus

Styracosaurus

Pachycephalosaurus

CRETACEOUS PERIOD 144 million years ago

The continents drifted further apart and split into smaller pieces. The dinosaurs were stranded on specific bits of land and evolved into more distinct regional types. Fast-growing, flowering plants began to appear that could support huge herds of grazing plant-eaters.

THE SECRET OF THEIR SUCCESS...

Unlike other reptiles, which splay their legs out when they move, dinosaurs had straight legs tucked underneath their bodies. This meant they could carry themselves more easily, run faster, grow bigger and walk further.

Reptile

Dinosaur

TWO LEGS OR FOUR?

Some dinosaurs walked on two legs and some on four. A few dinosaurs walked on two legs, but dropped down onto four to drink or browse for food.

Iguanadon

MONSTER MEAT-EATERS

The dense Mesozoic forest echoes with the sound of thunderous roars, tearing flesh and crunching bones. The ferocious meat-eating dinosaurs are on the rampage. With their slashing jaws, deadly claws and long, powerful hind legs, these monsters are a nightmare come to life — lean, mean killing machines.

TOOLS FOR KILLING

MEGA BITES

The giant carnivore, T-Rex, had jaws so wide that if it lived today it could snap you up whole. It had large, jagged teeth, which meant it could rip off chunks of meat and swallow them whole.

CANNIBAL COELOPHYSIS

The slim, child-sized Coelophysis was one of the first dinosaurs. A small Triassic meat-eater, it had strong clawed hands to grab and hold on to its prey.

Coelophysis

DEADLY CLAW

Dromaeosaurus was as small as a child, but had a large, curved claw on each of its feet. When it grabbed its prey, the claw swept down quickly in a deadly stabbing motion.

HANDYHOOK

A fossil of Baryonyx was found with fish scales in the stomach. This suggests that it was a wader that killed and ate fish, spearing them with its huge, footlong curved claw.

BIRDLIKE BEAK

Gallimimus had no teeth, and its hands couldn't grasp things. Its long beak snapped up insects, eggs and small animals. It also probably sifted tiny bits of food from mud and water through comblike plates in its beak.

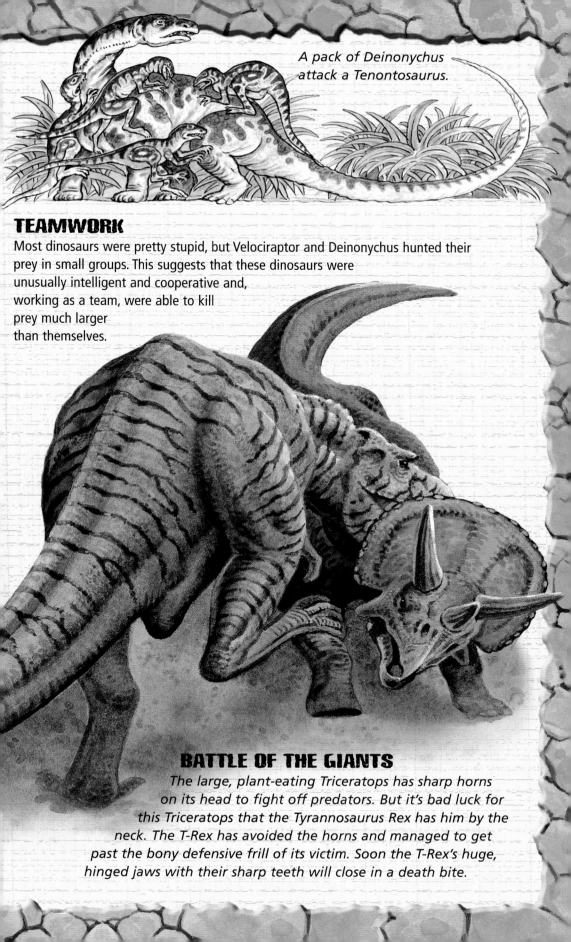

A pack of Deinonychus attack a Tenontosaurus.

TEAMWORK

Most dinosaurs were pretty stupid, but Velociraptor and Deinonychus hunted their prey in small groups. This suggests that these dinosaurs were unusually intelligent and cooperative and, working as a team, were able to kill prey much larger than themselves.

BATTLE OF THE GIANTS

The large, plant-eating Triceratops has sharp horns on its head to fight off predators. But it's bad luck for this Triceratops that the Tyrannosaurus Rex has him by the neck. The T-Rex has avoided the horns and managed to get past the bony defensive frill of its victim. Soon the T-Rex's huge, hinged jaws with their sharp teeth will close in a death bite.

VAST VEGETARIANS

On wooded plains, giant Brachiosaurus sniffs the air, searching for the tender treetop greenery that grows in the steamy Jurassic climate. Although these dinosaurs are enormous in size, they survive on a totally plant-based diet.

BODY ARMOUR

The peaceful plant-eaters were generally slow moving – easy prey for the fast-running meat-eaters. Some of them developed various types of body armour, such as thick skin, spikes and horns, for protection.

HEADS...

Triceratops   Centrosaurus

...OR TAILS

Euoplocephalus

Stegosaurus

The three powerful horns of Triceratops could inflict a fatal wound on an attacker. Spikes lining the bony neck frill of Centrosaurus looked fierce and gave extra protection.

Armour-plated Euoplocephalus had a huge, bony club at the end of its tail that it lashed from side to side. One blow would easily break the legs of an attacker. Stegosaurus likewise had a sharp, spiked tail for defence.

SAFETY IN NUMBERS

In the distance, a group of Apatosaurus is grazing at the muddy river mouth. These plant-eaters live in herds for protection. If a meat-eater threatens the herd, the adults shield their young and lash out at the attacker with their whip-like tails.

Brachiosaurus

Apatosaurus

CRESTED CORYTHOSAURUS

The Corythosaurus (left) had a thick crest of solid bone that, in males, might have been brightly coloured to attract a mate.

Corythosaurus

BEAKS...

Iguanodon

Pachycephalosaurus

Lambeosaurus

...AND CRESTS

Parasaurolophus

Iguanodon chopped off mouthfuls of leaves and twigs with its beak and ground them to a paste with its flat, back teeth. The teeth of Pachycephalosaurus were small, sharp and curved backwards, acting like a shredder.

Lambeosaurus had a hollow, axe-shaped crest on its head. Parasaurolophus could blow air through its long, hollow, bony crest to make a trumpeting noise.

DIGGING FOR DINOSAURS

In the heat of the desert sun, a fossil hunter uses a hammer and chisel to chip away at a rock face. After several hours, the imprint of a huge, wide, flat bone begins to appear. The hunter puts down his tools and takes a brush to clear away the powdery deposits. He has unearthed the fossil of a gigantic dinosaur shoulder blade. He lies down next to it; the single bone is taller than he is.

STAMPEDE!

At Lark Quarry in Australia, about 150 small dinosaurs gather around a waterhole. Suddenly, a large meat-eater approaches from the north, causing panic and a stampede. Scientists have been able to work this out from the mass of trackways left behind.

BONES
Great, wide columns of fossilised bone show the legs of a heavy giant. Hollow bones indicate a light runner. Gnaw marks on bones suggest which animal killed the dinosaur.

TEETH
Fossils of teeth show whether the dinosaur was a plant-eater or a meat-eater.

CLAWS
Fossilised claws indicate how certain types of meat-eater killed their prey.

WELL PRESERVED

In 1997, the almost complete skeleton of a T-Rex nicknamed Sue was auctioned and sold for US$7.6 million (£4 million). This T-Rex had died in a desert and dried out quickly without rotting. This meant that the body was mummified and softer body parts, such as skin and even folds in it, had been preserved.

DUEL TO THE DEATH

A freak sandstorm in the Mongolian desert buried two dinosaurs, a Velociraptor and a Protoceratops, as they fought to the death. The fossil remains show the Velociraptor in the process of killing the Protoceratops, slashing into its victim's belly with its foot-claw. But its forelimb is trapped in the Protoceratops' beaked jaws, so it cannot escape. The Protoceratops has also pierced the chest of the Velociraptor with the horn on its head.

FOOTPRINTS

Dinosaur footprints show whether dinosaurs walked on two or four legs. The footprints of large meat-eaters show they were lone hunters. Tracks of other types of dinosaur show they lived in herds. The adult animals may have protected their young from meat-eating predators by keeping them in the centre of the herd.

NESTS AND EGGS

Fossils of dinosaur eggs laid in nests on the ground indicate that certain types of dinosaur lived in herds that would return to the same nesting grounds each year.

DROPPINGS

Fossilised droppings often contain bits of the dinosaur's last meal, like seeds, pinecones or bones. The largest dropping ever found was from T-Rex, weighing 7kg (15lb).

DINOSAUR RECORD BREAKERS

For the biggest, smallest, fastest and brainiest dinosaurs ever, just look here!

BIGGEST TEETH

The fierce meat-eaters had enormous teeth – Allosaurus' were 10cm (4in) long, and T-Rex's were 20cm (8in) long.

LONGEST TAILS

The giant plant-eaters had long tails, to help balance the weight of their incredible necks. Seismosaurus' was the longest at 20m (65ft), then Diplodocus' 15m (50ft) and Apatosaurus' 11m (36ft).

Argentinosaurus – longest body 45m (150

Seismosaurus – longest tail 20m (65ft)

FASTEST RUNNERS

The fastest dinosaurs, Gallimimus, Ornithomimus and Struthiomimus, had strong back legs and could run 60-70km/h (35-40mph). They resemble, and were about the same size as, a modern ostrich. They had horny beaks and probably ate small animals, leaves and fruit.

SMALLEST DINOSAU

The smallest dinosaur was Compsognathus, a meat-eater only 60cm (2ft) from nose to tail.

Struthiomimus

Gallimimus

Compsognath

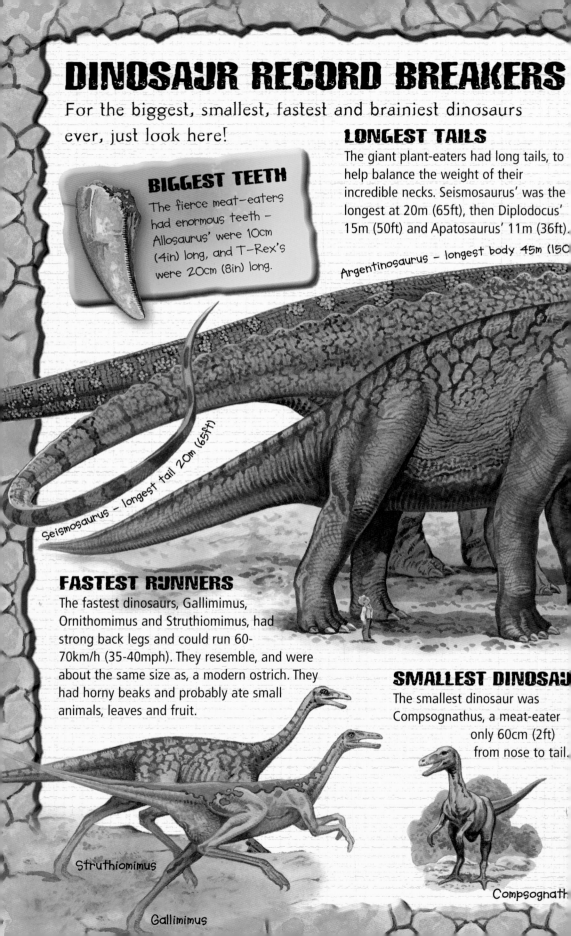